ENDA WALSH

Enda Walsh lives in London. He has had seven stage plays produced to date. These include *The Ginger Ale Boy*, *Disco Pigs*, *misterman* and *bedbound*. He has won the Stewart Parker and the George Devine Awards, two Edinburgh Fringe Awards and two Critic's Awards. *Disco Pigs* and *bedbound* have been translated into 18 languages and have had productions throughout Europe. His play *misterman* was in rep at the Schaubühne in Berlin for three years. He has written two radio plays: *Four Big Days in the Life of Dessie Banks* for RTE which won the IPA Radio Drama Award and *The Monotonous Life of Little Miss P* for the BBC which was commended at the Grand Prix Berlin. Recent plays include *The New Electric Ballroom* for the Kammerspiele in Munich and *Fraternity* for the Zürich Schauspielhaus. *Chatroom* was written for the National Theatre's Connections Project, and his play *Pondlife Angels* opened in Cork in June 2005. He wrote the screenplay of the film *Disco Pigs* which was released in 2002 and is currently under commission for two other films: *Miss Emerald Isle* and an adaptation of the children's story *The Island of the Aunts* by Eva Ibbotson. He is also working on a Bobby Sands Project for Film Four.

Other Titles in this Series

Simon Burt
BOTTLE UNIVERSE
GOT TO BE HAPPY

Jez Butterworth
MOJO
THE NIGHT HERON
THE WINTERLING

Caryl Churchill
BLUE HEART
CHURCHILL PLAYS: THREE
CHURCHILL: SHORTS
CLOUD NINE
A DREAM PLAY
    after Strindberg
FAR AWAY
HOTEL
ICECREAM
LIGHT SHINING IN
    BUCKINGHAMSHIRE
MAD FOREST
A NUMBER
THE SKRIKER
THIS IS A CHAIR
THYESTES *after* Seneca
TRAPS

Ariel Dorfman
DEATH AND THE MAIDEN
READER
THE RESISTANCE TRILOGY
WIDOWS

Debbie Tucker Green
BORN BAD
DIRTY BUTTERFLY
STONING MARY
TRADE & GENERATIONS

Ayub Khan-Din
EAST IS EAST
LAST DANCE AT DUM DUM
NOTES ON FALLING
    LEAVES

Tony Kushner
ANGELS IN AMERICA –
    PARTS ONE & TWO
HOMEBODY/KABUL

Jonathan Lichtenstein
THE PULL OF NEGATIVE
    GRAVITY

Iain F MacLeod
HOMERS
I WAS A BEAUTIFUL DAY

Owen McCafferty
CLOSING TIME
DAYS OF WINE AND ROSES
    after JP Miller
MOJO MICKYBO
SCENES FROM THE BIG
    PICTURE
SHOOT THE CROW

Conor McPherson
DUBLIN CAROL
McPHERSON: FOUR PLAYS
McPHERSON PLAYS: TWO
PORT AUTHORITY
SHINING CITY
THE WEIR

Arthur Miller
AN ENEMY OF THE PEOPLE
    after Ibsen
PLAYING FOR TIME

Mark O'Rowe
FROM BOTH HIPS &
    THE ASPIDISTRA CODE
HOWIE THE ROOKIE
MADE IN CHINA

Enda Walsh
DISCO PIGS
    & SUCKING DUBLIN
THE SMALL THINGS

bedbound
&
misterman

two plays by

ENDA WALSH

NICK HERN BOOKS
London
www.nickhernbooks.co.uk

A Nick Hern Book

bedbound and *misterman* first published in Great Britain in 2001
as a paperback original by Nick Hern Books, 14 Larden Road,
London W3 7ST

Reprinted 2006

bedbound and *misterman* copyright © 2001 by Enda Walsh

Typeset by Country Setting, Kingsdown, Kent CT14 8ES
Printed in Great Britain by CLE Print Ltd, St Ives, Cambs, PE27 3LE

A CIP catalogue record for this book is available from
the British Library

ISBN-13   978 1 85459 640 6
ISBN-10   1 85459 640 3

*These two plays are dedicated to the memory
of my wonderfully generous and very funny father*

Sean Walsh

I miss you

bedbound

Characters

DAD

DAUGHTER

bedbound was first performed at The New Theatre, eircom
Dublin Theatre Festival 2002, with the following cast:

DAD   Peter Gowen
DAUGHTER   Norma Sheahan

Director   Enda Walsh
Designer   Fiona Cunningham
Lighting Designer   John Gallagher
Sound Designer   Bell Helicopter

It was subsequently performed at the Royal Court Jerwood
Theatre Upstairs, London, on 10 January 2002, with the
following cast change:

DAD   Liam Carney

*There is a large box in the centre of the stage made out of
plaster board. Suddenly the wall facing the audience crashes
to the ground. A light comes up on a small child's bed inside
the box. It is heavily stained and grubby. On one end of the
bed is a young woman. She is the* DAUGHTER. *Her back is
twisted and we can see that she is obviously crippled. Her face
is filthy, her hair tangled and manky. On the other end of the
bed facing her is her* DAD. *He is a large fifty-year-old man.
He wears a suit which is soiled and creased. He is pale and
ill looking. His face and hair are cleaner than hers giving the
impression that she has been in the bed much longer than him.
With the upstage wall on the ground the bed is now surrounded
on three sides by plasterboard walls. There is a small window
high on one of the side walls but the glass has been painted
black. The bed is covered in a dirty floral duvet. When the
wall falls the* DAUGHTER *looks out to the audience. She is
completely lifeless.*

DAUGHTER. I'm in the bed. The panic has sucked me dry
again 'til all that's left is ta start over. I get that tiredness
turn to tight . . . and I give in ta the words. I let go. Go.

DAD *explodes and performs a story from his childhood.*

DAD. FUCK FUCK FUCK FUCK FUCK FUCK fucking hell
fucking hell fuck fuck fuck Jesus fuck!! Fucking hell!! DAN
DAN!! Me in the bed. I can feel these blankets like a big sea
and me a little shrimp ways underneath!! Feel them wrapped
around me bony body ribs making me stay in the bed. Squeeze
me lungs out of me gob making me shout, 'Fucking hell get
out of the bed, Maxie!! You're late!!' I swing me legs out of
the bed already running I run inta tha jacks! There's me big
brother Gerry on the jacks having an early morning crap!!
I smack him a left hook!! Shmack!! He hits the ground like
the sack of shit he is!! 'I'll deal with you later, kiddo!'
Splish splash run the tap and get scrubbing me face!!

DAD *and* DAUGHTER. Gotta be clean!! Havta look sharp!

DAD. Look in the mirror at the fifteen-year-old me looking
back! 'Gotta get to work, Maxie! Only fourteen seconds to
save the planet Earth, Flash!' Spin back to the bedroom and
into the suit!! A bit damp from washing it last night but
fuck it! Isn't it always damp from its late night wash!? Have
ta be clean! Gotta get going! Inta the wet shirt! On with the
damp suit! Jesus I'm the smart one! Sharp is what I am!!
Outta my smelly hole gaff, the stink of the hot sweet milk
in the air, a breakfast puke! A family of lazy fucks huddled
around the electric heater like laboratory rats, I leave the
fucks behind. Shame shame!! Fucking shame!! I'm at the
bus-stop! Bus stops and I'm on! The usual faces stuck in
their morning sleep! 'Great workers of Ireland! Is it not
time to drag this priest-ridden, second-rate, potato-peopled
country of ours into the 20th century before we're spat into
the next shagging hundred years?' They half-smile back like
I'm a fucking psycho! Fuck em! I sit down in my usual
spot!! Twitching twitching 'cause I gotta be there! Gotta be
at work. Bus stops and I'm running. My damp suit tight
around my legs like glue almost! I see the shop. Stop dead
still and breathe it all in. Read the sign on the pearly gates.
'Robson's Furniture Emporium'. I'm fifteen and I'm
working. But working in the storeroom!!

DAUGHTER. That fucking suit! Didn't I tell ya ta wear something scruffy, ya uppidy bollix!

DAD. I ignore the storeroom boss, Eugene, a great big ball of
sweat with trousers hanging off his damp arse wanting to be
free of it all. I stay silent and work! The furniture all
wrapped up in plastics and paper, I get working!

DAUGHTER. Good lad!

DAD. Shifting the stock around like chess pieces. Vans pull up
to the big corrugated door which snaps open! A great big
hungry mouth and us the little storeroom hungry tongues
gobbling up the furniture and packing them away!! But I'm
the hungriest tongue of all 'cause I love the fucking work!!

DAUGHTER. He loves the fucking work!

DAD. Work work work work work work work work!!!
Satisfuckinfaction boys satisfuckinfaction! Fat Eugene calls

DAUGHTER. Teabreak!

DAD. . . . and out with the tabloids and teabags!! Fuck that!!
I sit alone! My damp suit steaming steam off it! Sit with me
little notebook marked 'Enemies' and jot down all the bad
things they throw in my direction!! Eugene's cavernous
mouth spewing out the funny talk.

DAUGHTER (*punchline*). Shiny knob!! I'll give ya a shiny
knob! (*Roars laughing, stops and growls.*) Ya Prince
fucking Charles.

DAD. Fat Eugene fucking hates me, boy. Wait 'til you're the
boss, Maxie-lad! By fuck there'll be some arses kicked
then, boys.

DAUGHTER. Right lads!

DAD. And head down I work and work and work and work!!
And my body like some slick machine and my brain keen
and fast!! I rise up the stairs from the storeroom. I feel its
blackness on my back leave as I step onto the sales floor.
And all colour returns as the beautiful cabinets and couches
stretch out in front of me on the blue baise. I watch the
salesmen at their work. I look at their easy manner and
stand as they chat 'comfort' to the customers. Like royalty
they look or something. Their hands barely touching the
fine fabrics and polished tables as they waltz around the
store to a music inside their heads. I take out my other
notebook marked, 'Salesman' and jot it all down. I watch
the eyes of the customers oohhhing and ahhing as the
salesman lays on the superlatives, spinning out the patter
that crackles in the air. I listen to the humour of the sales
floor reeling in the wallets, adding the V-A-T and tickling
the tills. I watch the teary eyes of the salesman as he waves
a lost sale goodbye . . . only to turn on his heels all hungry
and smiling as he spies a couple slouch inta a three-piece
suite. I write the words, 'This will all be mine. One day',
and I feel a horn battle against my damp pants to be free.
What a fucking beginning, boy! By fuck Cork I'll lay ye out

and fla the hole off ya!! Oh yes!! Bring it on boys. Bring it on! Is there no end to me?! Is there no end to me, tell me?! For have I not arrived Dan Dan!! Have I not arrived Dan Dan!! DAN DAN!! DAN DAN!! DAN DAN!! DAN DAN!! DAN DAN!!

DAD *panics and falls to the bed. The* DAUGHTER *begins to panic.*

DAUGHTER. He stops/it stops/his panic putting an end to him and a start to me/I see that silence/oh Christ/fill it fast!/feel it race towards me all full of the lonliness/think fast of of of of of/my body!/my body ache is what I feel now/that fills my head/that packs the silence with the smell of dust and piss/but my body ache is . . . /my curvy back!/the walls are still and silent with no thump pa de thump any more/they just stand looking down on me and him/it was me and she/but she is dead/I watch my Mam die, ya know/get the words in my head/they line up/I feel the words line up and use my mouth like a cliff edge/they jump/fall fast with an ugly-scream/my body ache/the smell of piss and shit/stunted and twisted girl/mouth an angry hole/me the dust mite is what I am/I can feel me sit in me and must know that this is my body/but no control/mouth like a cliff edge/body a thick duvet lump/smelling my body smell/all stale/give a little puke then/watch the puke take to the duvet where once was flowers but now all muck/all is muck and dust/he stops his big talk and I see a silence that needs packing with words/oh christ/calm/'calm' is a small word ya can't shout/calm is what I want/I ask my head for 'calm'/my head gets all blocked with muck/must think fast then/try to think through the muck inside my head/why did I think of muck?/mustn't think of muck anymore/must think of 'sky' so to open my head and speak out lots of other words/the word 'sky' breaks through the muck and gives me 'blue' and 'space' and 'white clouds' and 'summers'/my head sets free on images I can't talk of/too big they are/but it brings me some little ease not to be speaking with words and just lying in the picture of a blue sky dotted in clouds/not to be thinking of the muck/not to be thinking of the bed/the fucking bed/my life my life my life/think fast/the sky and

clouds fold inta the grey and pack inta a box marked
'muck'/fuck it!/so I try to think of my name/what is my
name?/did she call me my name?/she called me Princess.
I watched her die/I'm a child/no!/I'm a woman/I *was* a
child/I was ten/I'm a woman/what is ten and ten?/could it
be ten years?/ten years of me and her in the bed/what is the
banging, Mam?, I ask/the walls are getting closer?/what
makes the walls getting closer?, I ask/ it's a fairytale, she
says/we are in a fairytale/we're waiting for a Prince/wait for
the Prince, love/wait for his kiss/wait for his kiss/ten years
and we wait for the Prince/we get *him*/he calls himself Dad/
says he's my Dad/is he my Dad?, I ask the walls/but the
walls don't answer 'cause the walls are dead and silent/the
bastards/all full of the big talk is what he is/I remember my
Dad as a shadow and a voice/now I want for the shadow
back/I face his ugly mush and showered with spit and tooth
decay for a week now it seems/with his big talk/all full of
the big talk/I get his story of furniture and then know he
must be my Dad/'furniture' my whole life up until the walls
banging/the walls are getting closer/but I fill the silence and
let him talk and I act out this Dan Dan and Sparkey and all
the men/for what am I if I'm not words?/I'm empty space is
what I am/what am I if I'm not words I'm empty space/so
I learn the men and play them big/we fill the room with
what he was until he stops/he stops/looks all afraid and tries
to sleep/like it were some nightmare or something/and him
just remembering this dream life of his/but a nightmare it
seems/that story of Dublin/of dirty Dublin Dan Dan!/which
gets me at the book/ (*She pulls out a worn filthy softback
novella.*) this book that Mam did read and opened up a story
of colour/a story outside of the bed/outside of the room/
outside in the outside/a story of romance/I watched my
Mam die so I must now read alone/can I read this story as
she did?/my big question is can I read the story as Mam
did?/and fear won't let me try/'cause maybe I can't/afraid to
start to read/but I must/and I have to read as she did and
find that place again, don't I?/to break free/to get free/to be
free as she and me did/to be out/to be outside of this/to not
have to think/but to allow a story of love to take me up/to
set me free/of this/of him/of me.

DAD. SHUT THE FUCK UP!!

DAUGHTER. I CAN'T!

DAD. I'm trying to sleep!!

DAUGHTER. What's the point!! You should talk to me. Why don't we talk? Ya stopped talking to me!

DAD. I tried talking to ya, ya stumpy bitch!

DAUGHTER. Well try again!

DAD. I want to sleep!

DAUGHTER. You won't be able to sleep.

DAD. I won't be able while we're talking, so shut the fuck up!

DAUGHTER. You won't be able when it's silent! You should face up to it! We're awake and that's the way it is in here!

DAD. I've got nothing to talk to you about.

DAUGHTER. We're talking now!

DAD. Yeah but about nothing!

DAUGHTER. It's filling the gaps, isn't it?!

DAD. It's making the gaps! If we didn't talk there would be no gaps! There'd be quiet! A great big field of quiet! That's what I want!

DAUGHTER. We can't have quiet!

DAD. Well I could!

DAUGHTER. Don't!

DAD. I could! Talking is what *you* want! I want sleep! I'm not here for you, ya know! (*He goes to get out of the bed.*)

DAUGHTER. Don't go!

DAD. *I* can walk!

DAUGHTER. Don't!

DAD. I could!

DAUGHTER. Don't!

DAD. I could do what I want! My legs are in great shape!

DAUGHTER. Don't!

DAD. You fuck! You little bollix! It just crept up on me! Ya got me talking about something when talking to you is the fucking last thing on my mind! You've got the words bubbling up from inside me and making me spit out and talk, ya little puke! Now I've started I can't stop!

DAUGHTER. We both can't stop! That's all part of it!

DAD. It? What the fuck is 'it'?

DAUGHTER *(giggling)*. Me, you, the bed, time!

DAD. Both of us have stopped!

DAUGHTER. But not at the same time!!

DAD. I'll fucking stop! I'll rip me tongue out!

DAUGHTER. Ya wouldn't!

DAD. I could chew it off! I could tear me ears off me head and get some sleep! Find some rest! Let you do the talking!

DAUGHTER. Ya wouldn't do that!

DAD. The point is, I could! I could do it and then who would ya talk to? And what do you mean I wouldn't? What makes you know what I would or wouldn't do Dan Dan? I fucking will, ya cheeky cunt! *(He begins to chew his tongue. He screams.)* Yarrah fuck!!

DAUGHTER *laughs.*

DAD. You're making me leave!

DAUGHTER. Don't!

DAD. I can go! *(His mouth bleeds.)*

DAUGHTER. No don't!

DAD. The point is I might! The point is I might go! The point is the point is . . . *(Slight pause.)* I'm bleeding!

DAUGHTER. What?

DAD (*devastated*). I'm alive. (*Pause.*) I'm still alive. Fuck.

DAUGHTER (*to herself, delighted*). I'm alive!

DAD (*he shouts*). Back back back back back . . .

DAUGHTER (*overlapping*). Back back back back back back . . . (*She laughs.*)

DAD (*overlapping*). . . . baCK BACK BACK BACK BACK MAXIE!!! I stand in my damp tight suit, my fifteen-year-old hands twitching twitching twitching, my eyes fixed calm on Mr. Bee. It seens only him stands between me and my destiny. I watch his seventy-year-old baggy suit and hound-dog eyes standing in the ke ke ke ke ke kitchen department like some sad museum piece.

DAD. Give him a Maxie smile. Nice.

DAUGHTER. Ya know, Maxie, but ya ke ke ke ke keep that suit looking lo lo lovely.

DAD. 'Ah thanks, Mr. Bee. Are ya ready to head home then?' We stand at the bus stop. And then in the bus and I listen to the stories he patches together with the phrase,

DAUGHTER. And another fu funny thing . . .

DAD. I smile the smile of a friend. Truth is I hate the dusty fucker. I hate his soft old ways, his tatty photo of his dead wife Pa pa pa pa pa Peggy, those grease proof wrapped sandwiches all sweaty and thick with butter, that morning tradition he has of sitting in the shop ca ca ca ca ca canteen smoking a lucky cigar before the shop door opens. I hate him all. But I smile though. I learn everything about him and when I go home I jot it down in a notebook marked,

DAD *and* DAUGHTER. 'How to k k k k k kill Mr. B B B B B Bee'.

DAD. He tells me he's lost his sense of smell. I draw a star beside it and send myself to sleep whispering 'destiny' over and over and over. Next day he answers his doorbell. 'All right, Mr. Bee, ready for the off then?!'

DAUGHTER. Good to see ya, Ma Maxie! Step in, son.

DAD. He waddles back into the kitchen. I follow. I run the tap for a glass of water but fill it with paraffin. I turn all clumsy and whoops-a-daisy, I spill the paraffin all over Mr. Bee's jacket sleeves and lucky cigar which peeps out from his breast pocket like a shy little doggy. 'Just water!' I say to Mr. Bee's odourly challanged no no no no no no nose.

DAUGHTER. Sure let it da dry, then!

DAD. We arrive at Robson's Furniture Emporium, me worn with his endless drivelling, him drenched in paraffin ithing for his morning ci ci ci ci ci cigar. I watch as he places the cigar in his mouth and roots for his matches. Watch his cocktail sausage fingers fumble the matchbox like it were a large snot. I turn and hear the click of the match off the box. I hear the tear of the strike. And I walk from the small canteen for the storeroom as Mr. Bee explodes into 'fla fla flames' and lights my future upwards. (*Slight pause.*) He loved his butter, Mr. Bee. By fuck he was burning for five hours, boy! And I mean, who would have believed it? (*Laughs.*) I'm a saleman. (*Screams.*) Dan Dan!! Dan Dan?? DAN DAN MY FUCK WIT VAN MAN!!

DAUGHTER. I'm here boss, I'm here!

DAD. For fuck sake man!! Aren't these gone yet!

DAUGHTER. They're gone now! They're on the way!! They're in the van!!

DAD. They're fucking in front of me, Dan Dan!! What's the fucking point of me selling the shagging things if they're left here to gather dust!! It's not ours now so fucking get a move on!

DAUGHTER. We're working hard, boss!

DAD. Don't tell me what work is, Dan Dan!! Who the fuck are ye ta tell me that! You're only a snivelling lazy cunt with less sense than a stupid fucking donkey! You're a fucking stupid donkey-man, Dan Dan!! (DAUGHTER *makes the noise of a donkey.*) There's a science documentary in you Mister Donkey-Man!!

DAUGHTER. You're a gas man, boss!

DAD. Where the fuck is Fat Eugene?

DAUGHTER. In the stores, boss!

DAD. Send the fat fucker up here!! I need something to punch!

DAUGHTER. Ya called boss!!

DAD (*punches*). 'Schmack!!'

DAUGHTER. I'll clear him up will I, boss?

DAD. Tell him he's fired when he comes around. When I was fifteen, lads, that fat fuck stank my air real bad. Like working with a giant poo poo always hanging around.

DAUGHTER. Ah very funny, boss!

DAD. And Dan Dan!

DAUGHTER. Yes, boss.

DAD. You watch your back yerself or I'll tear lumps outta a ya, boy!

DAUGHTER. Fair enough!!

DAD. 'Now move it!!' Twenty three and Robson's Furniture Emporium dances to my beat. I keep a book marked 'Customers'. I know where they live. I visit their locals in the evenings. I call into the pub and . . . 'Jesus, Danny, how's tricks!! That wall unit working out fine, is it?! No I won't have a . . . ah give us a mineral so!'

DAD *and* DAUGHTER. Another pub another sale . . .

DAD. 'Seamus! How are ya?! Wa ya ya a halla a wha?!' I know everything about them. Before they know it they're chatting personals in the pub jacks, 'Ya'd wanta get that mole seen to, Robbie! By fuck that doesn't look healthy at all!!!!' I fit in sixteen pubs a night! Now that's stamina! Sundays and I'm doing the rounds on the football pitches! Cheering for my customers, being their best friend. 'Great shot, Trevor!! Good man!!' I sit in Bingo halls and chat recipes with the old ladies during the interval. I learn off the recipes and spout them out! What do I know about food and cookery?!

DAD *and* DAUGHTER. Couldn't give a bollix me!

DAD. But then I slip in, 'Jesus, ya should see the colourful work tops we've got, girls! Magic!!'

DAUGHTER. I'll pop in tomorrow so!

DAD. And it's all worthwhile. Robson's is my success! Mine alone! Twenty three and Cork is mine! I'm loved by them! But the point is! I mean the point is they're spending their cash in my shop!! (*Screams.*) Dan Dan!!

DAUGHTER. Yeah boss!!

DAD. What's the problem, boy?!

DAUGHTER. We need an extra pair of hands, boss.

DAD. 'Get out of the fucking way so!' I take the three-seater in my arms like a new born baby and sling it in the back of the van. Join the three van men by way of supervision. 'Who the fuck are you?'

DAUGHTER. Terry.

DAD. How long have you been with us, Gary?

DAUGHTER. Two years now!

DAD. Two years? Well shift your hole for the boss. How are you then, Sparkey?

DAUGHTER. Tops, boss!!

DAD. Jesus you're one ugly fucker! Married are ya?

DAUGHTER. Not yet, boss.

DAD. I wouldn't hold your breath, Sparkey boy! D'ya know sick people would pay good money to see a face like yours.

DAUGHTER. Ah yer a gas man, boss!

DAD. 'Drive on Dan Dan!!' And off we go. I feel the tension hang in the air. I stare ahead sensing their grubby hands pumping out the sweat. Just waiting for my roars. They hate me. Do I give a fuck? Do I bollix!

DAUGHTER. That's Mrs. Dexter's there, boss!!

DAD. 'Well get a fucking move on.' I stand on the kerb
surveying the three stooges grapple with the wall unit like it
were made out of clitoris. 'Get your back into it, Sparkey.'
We enter Mrs. Dexter's gate and up through her garden as
pristeen as anything ya'd see on the telly. Fine roses them.
Fancy-floral. Lovely. 'Mrs. Dexter, Eileen! We've arrived!
Early as usual! Step aside, love, and we'll get the job done.'

DAUGHTER. Ya'll have a cup a tea, will ya?!

DAD. A cup of tea! Ah now don't be spoiling these fellas!
Sure they don't even know what tea is!!

DAUGHTER. Very funny, boss!!

DAD. No fucking mistakes now.

DAUGHTER. All right, lads! Easy now, Sparkey!

DAD. I imagine the pressure on Dan Dan's tiny brain as he
leads the wall unit between the straights of Mrs. Dexter's
doorway. His light blue eyes unblinking begin to seep sweat
and glisten from his grubby little face. I watch his thick
fingers like . . . like chicken drumsticks bend around the
wall unit. The veins on his head balloon with thick
cholesterol and my voice. His back, the size of a horse's,
inches further and further into the house. For a second,
probably less, I feel what amounts to a tiny pride as Dan
Dan and his idiot helpers place the wall unit against Mrs.
Dexter's sitting room wall. Oh very good. Very very good.
(*Screams.*) 'TAKE YOUR FUCKING TIME, WHY DON'T
YA!' (*Calmly to audience.*) No matter how often you
remind someone that you're the boss . . . it can never be
enough, believe me boy. (*Screams.*) 'Ah for fuck sake, Dan
Dan, YA FUCKING RETARD!!'

DAUGHTER. What is it, boss?

DAD *begins to panic a bit and covers himself with a
blanket. The* DAUGHTER *is immediately nervous.*

DAUGHTER. Is that all we're doing then? Daddy? Dad?

The silence closes in on the DAUGHTER *and she begins to
panic. She looks at the book and braces herself to read it.*

She begins to read but is beginning to lose it as the words spin out of control.

DAUGHTER. Katie was small with delicate bones and an air of vulnerability that drew men to her like bees to honey. Across the massive ballroom the light from the chandelier speckled down on débutantes as they cavorted with one another. Handsometall mentheir long backs and angular jawlines seemed dull and dreadfully vain to Katie otheryoungwomen with wanton eyes and . . . oh Christ . . . and and and poutinglipspositionedthemselvesaroundthevasthall, like dead mannequins, Katie thought. For fuck sake calm calm calm calm . . . for although angelicandserene inappearanceKatie'smindhousedawickedwit . . . oh fuck/ I know it so well!/each word I know is stuck in her voice/ a voice I can't speak/I feel my head panic and reach out to get to the next sentence/I feel that sentence fall away from me/I see the calm face of my Mam/she reads the book and the words not fire but pass with a music from her voice/my voice so ugly/but must keep talking to fill this fucking silence!/is this it?/already I'm living some manky future with him of the big talk and me of the fast/me scuttering words like a sick arse/him crashing the words about/bruising the air!/ohh fuck this/fill it fill it fill it fill it FILL IT/think of Katie/ (*Blocks her eyes.*) look through the grey and think of Katie in the book/her skin!/I see her skin!/'delicate' is what they say/'ivory' is how they say it/and on a horse/her hair 'whipped by the wind' as she goes faster and faster/and the landscape 'lush' and pastoral/try to place me there I make the lush all damp and old dust/fuck/fill it fill it/forget me to be her/and Katie in her room/all big as she watches the light on her face as she hears his voice from the study below/and lipstick/and something in her eye/some 'cunning'/and her mother/Katie's mother/so beautiful she is/she calls/he's waiting in the study/she calls with a 'cheeky' voice/and there's laughter in my Mam's voice as she reads/and I can see Katie smile/good fuck/my fucking life/I can see her stand and walk/her lightness/the sun leaving her back as she faces her future with him/her future/while mine is all deadened/all twisted/all sad/all fucking bad/I can't feel the book, Mam!/Jesus holy fuck!

DAD *sits up and watches her screaming, crying. He shows no sympathy for her. He looks like he may even laugh.*

DAUGHTER. What did ya do to Mam?

He doesn't answer.

DAUGHTER. Are you really my Dad?

DAD *breathes in deep and takes off once more.*

DAD (*screaming triumphant*). EUROPE DAN DAN!!

DAUGHTER (*overlapping*). Answer it!

DAD (*overlapping*). Hotel dining room, furniture delegates breakfasting on muesli and fucking yogurt! 'Jeez I'd murder a sausage sangwidge' but steer my energies towards progress! I'm sharp! A new suit marks me out from the rest!

DAUGHTER (*screams*). Answer it!!

DAD. 'Good morning, gentleman!! Bon jour as they say!!' Before I know it I'm chomping through a thing called a croissant, swigging a black coffee and acting more Continental than Sacha Distel! 'You've gotta be ahead a the pack to try patent shoes but you know Richard, my English friend, I've got two words for you 'Dirk' 'Bogart'. Granted he was a steamer but what a dresser!!' Talking to some Norwegian bloke called Lars I hear his new line in wardrobes and dining-room tables are A-one! 'Well that sounds like I might be interesting in that, Lars!!' Trouble is everyone fucking knows! 'Sorry Richard! Can I have a word in your ear, Lars?' Out with the francs and me and my buddy Lars kicking our way through a Paris Springtime! Into some classy strip place and Lars sucking at the end of a bottle of Champagne. He fucking loves me boy! 'I can tell that yer a right little goer, hey Larsie?!' I call over two slappers and slip them a few hundred! Before I know it me and Lars and the two slappers are rolling around a giant bed with the hungriest genitals in Gay Paree! Suddenly it stops! Lars tells the girls to fuck off and then faces me! In perfect English he asks me to bend over, that he wants to lick my arse. I face the pillow and feel the wet tongue tickle my crack . . . reminding me that the last time I took a shit it was courtesy of British Airways. He then assumes the position and asks for a good licking himself. I face his hairy hole and what stares back at me . . . what stares back at me are the faces of my competitors rapt in jealousy. (*He licks.*) The deal is mine, Dan Dan.

DAUGHTER. You're a marvel, boss.

DAD. You better believe it, boy. Now get those fucking wasters Terry and Sparkey to unload the new merchandise.

The DAUGHTER*'s playing of the characters is tougher now. Like she's pushing him.*

DAUGHTER. My wife thinks the world of you, boss.

DAD. She's a wise woman. In some respects.

DAUGHTER. Ever think of getting a wife yourself?

DAD. A wife? And what the fuck would I be needing with a wife?

DAUGHTER. To do the cooking, boss.

DAD. And by fuck but Dan Dan was making some sense! Recalling a young quiet thing who clung to her Mam in the Bingo Hall, I make my moves. I spot her reading some romantic tacky book. Clear my throat to be heard above the bingo scribbling, my first words are, 'You should marry me, you know'.

DAUGHTER. Congratulations, boss!

DAD. 'Why thanks very much Dan Dan!' I enroll her in an evening class entitled 'Create your own Dinner Parties'. Each month the house packed with vol-au-vents and fields upon fields of cocktail sausages. Pastry clogging her hands like sticky winter mittens, for fuck sake!! Mister and misses me and her. Her done up like a porcelain doll, me like a life-sized action man! What a team! I invites my best customers! They fucking love me!

DAUGHTER. Jesus, Maxie, but this is a great spread!

DAD. You should see the new Norweeeegen range in the bedding department, Bernard! Such bargains!

DAUGHTER. My God, but you've transformed the city!

DAD. And he's right! I've done it all. It's all my doing. Take another cheesy vol-au-vent, Bernard, plenty more from where that came from, boy!' (*He laughs. Pause. Tone turns grave.*) Then I spy 'him'. A new face. A face all tanned and handsome. A suit of light grey and loose. A laugh of a rich man. He walks towards me his eyes slowly smiling then. His long hand closing around my squatty fingers.

DAUGHTER. I'm a friend of Bernard's. Marcus Enright.

DAD. I feel the name etch its way through my head and sit behind the back of my eyes and know already that I will never be free of that name. Marcus Enright. An ex-barrister, he tells me he's going to open a furniture shop in Dublin. How his two sons share his interest in

DAUGHTER. Quality furniture.

DAD. I fucking hate him. I want to open his face with the corkscrew I carry around. Want to drag him on to our new patio and barbecue the posh bollix. He's making me feel cheap. I watch him flinch as he lowers the Blue Nun from his mouth. I vow to see his business fucked. I promise to gobble him up and shit him out. Fuck it, I need an ally though!

DAUGHTER (*her own voice*). Ya need a son!

DAD. I go at the wife all doggy style. Grabbing her round arse in my prawn cocktail stained hands with the dinner party and no doubt Marcus fucking Enright in full swing down below. It's my first ever fuck. Never had the time, interest, want before until now. My tiny prick grapples to make its mark. Like sky diving into a giant sky called 'fanny', like throwing a ball up Patrick's Street, like getting up on the Shannon Estuary, I jiggle about for all of two minutes before I shoot my load. 'Never doubt the potency of my sperm, woman!' Nine months later and it's all push push pushing! 'Til out it drops! Not a son at all but a girl!

DAUGHTER. Hello Dad!

DAD. Fuck! Undaunted I get her reading baby books on her first goo gaa! Books about furniture! Pop-up books about chairs and tables. Her first word,

DAUGHTER. Stool.

DAD. 'Ah that's excellent, sweety!' Her first drawing,

DAUGHTER (*like a baby*). A chest of drawers.

DAD. Dan Dan, my daughter!

DAUGHTER. She's beautiful, boss!

DAD. She's a fucking genius, man, don't mind that beauty stuff. Looks fade, boy! She takes after her old man. Time for a new sign on the old shop, Dan Dan. Fuck that Robson's Furniture Emporium bollix. From now on it's Maxwell Darcy and Daughter.

DAUGHTER. Maxwell Darcy and Daughter?

DAD. Happy days, Dan Dan. Happy days!

DAUGHTER (*her own voice, hard*). I don't remember them, Dad.

DAD *begins to panic.*

DAUGHTER. I'll speak the only thing that's clear to me just ta shut you out. I remember I fire meself out of this bed and sling my ten-year-old bikini on.

DAD *tries to hide under the blanket. She continues with conviction.*

DAUGHTER. It's all yellow with pink dots and I fasten it around my chest . . . as if I had anything to hide. I've got awful problems fastening the bikini but then feel the long fingers of Mam click me into shape and pat me on the head. I smell the hand cream on her fingers. I look at her fingers made rough from all the pastry. All those millions of vol-au-vents turning her hands to cake. All for you and that fucking shop. I tell her that she's beautiful because to me she is. As usual she stays quiet and we get the bus to the beach with the Summer heat sending the bus shimmering towards our stop. 'Might Dad one day blow up, Mam?' I think that was the question I asked. And she started to laugh. The people on the bus turned and smiled because her laugh was so loud and happy. I had a good old laugh meself thinking of you blowing up in our new fitted kitchen all over the Formica work tops. In my laugh I let a fart which made Mam laugh even louder. All laughed out we lay in the water as the tide tippled up over us and both looking up towards the sun. Scrunched up faces. I turned over and lay on Mam and kissed the salt off her face. The dry sea salt on her beautiful face like she were a frosted bun I told her. And then she hugged me so hard it almost squeezed the air out of my inflatable swan ring. That was nice. And that's when I went for a walk. I left Mam lying on the beach. That would be the last time I would see her as a healthy girl. I walked over the dunes spying on the teenagers snatching at their crotches. I talked to a priest sunbathing with the Bible and his crippled mother who sucked on oranges like they were going out of fashion. He read the story about Jesus in the desert to me and squatted a wasp with the Gospel of Saint John. Squished it dead. I walked on pretending that I was Jesus in search of water with only hours to live. I pretended I was a desert rabbit and ran through the sharp rushes like a right mad yoke. The rushes like nasty pins and needles firing me faster and faster and faster and faster. The soft sand sent spitting from my heels. My skinny arms and legs a mad blur. My springy hair springing out straight from my speed. My head free. Free of you and that fucking furniture talk. And then I felt no ground underneath me. Like the dog in the Roadrunner cartoons I tried running in the air. It was sort of funny until I fell down. And I fell down into this big hole. And right up to my waist I was covered in shit. I soon stopped trying to catch any clean air and just breathed in the shit air. I had a little puke. Puked up the cola bottles I ate on the bus. I wiped my mouth of the puke with a hand covered in shit. I spat the shit out and started to climb up a little ladder out of the concrete hole. And I didn't even cry. And that's the story of the day I got the polio. From then on everything went mad, didn't it? And ya know a day doesn't go past where I think I should have stayed in that place. How fucking happy I'd be.

The DAD *is speechless. It is clear that he has been touched by the beauty of her story.*

DAUGHTER. Why is it that's a clear picture and nothing else is? Do you have any answers for me, Dad?

DAD. I don't know what anything is. Everything's all fucked up.

DAUGHTER. Then speak of Dublin then, Dad! Speak of Dublin but don't get all afraid like before and just speak up until right this moment, Dad . . . right this moment for me. Just let go and say it as it was! Let go, Maxie! Let go! Let go! (*Overlapping.*) GO GO GO GO GO GO GO GO GO GO GO GO!!!!

Using her energy he throws himself into his days in Dublin.

DAD (*overlapping*). 'Fuck fuck fuck fuck fuck fuck fuck fucking hell fucking hell fuck fuck fuck Jesus fuck!! Fucking hell!! Dan Dan!!' DUBLIN!! DIRTY DUBLIN!

DAUGHTER (*as herself*). Jesus Maxie, I can't see it working! The shops in rag order!

DAD (*under serious pressure*). I'll be the judge of that! Am I not the boss?! Is this not the boss stuck right in front of ya, ya fucking Dublin cunt!?

DAUGHTER. It's too expensive for our clientèle! We haven't a chance to shift it, Maxie!

DAD. 'Listen to me ya little college shite! The fact a the matter is . . . the fact a the matter is . . . I mean the fact a the matter is . . . arrah fuck Schmackkk! Brian pick him up and fuck him out! Get yer backs into it lads! This is history! What man has opened three furniture shops on the same day throughout Dublin!? What man? Answer me that Marcus Enright? Answer me that, you of the tight hole!! No fucking, man! No fucking Jackeen, either lads! Sure doesn't it take a Cork man to build! God himself was from Glasheen! He fucking well was boys! Knew him well! By Christ, God was a worker!! Work work work! Continents were born! Work a bit harder the seas were flowing! Scratched his arse and out popped Britain! By fuck I have ya Dublin! Ya arrogant little pup! Eleven o'clock and these doors swing open, Brian! Swing open!' I leave the shop! The muscles on me neck

showing off those pumping veins like a thick cock! I turn
and read the sign! 'Maxie's Furniture Super Shop'! A flash
of you pictures in me head with your twisted body soaked
in the polio! SHIT!! SHIT!! I walk! I walk through Dublin!
I feel the power in my body! I could have driven but
walking is more powerful, isn't it? Walking is where it's at,
boys!! Like a great big battleship I walk the length of O'
Connell Street towering over the Dublin scum. 'Jesus, yer
not so uppidy now, are ya?! Not now that Maxie's in town!
Three shops in one day! A fucking record man!' I swing
onto Parnell Street with the power of a planet, the grace of a
movie star, the Michael Collins of the furniture world! And
there!! And there are the cameras!! Photographers piled up
outside Maxie's Furniture Super Shop Number Two!
Waiting! Waiting for the one and only! Waiting for the man
himself!!

Cameras flashing.

DAD. Jesus thanks for coming, lads!

DAUGHTER. Congratulations, Maxie.

DAD. Thanks son, thanks!

DAUGHTER. Fantastic shop, Maxie!

DAD. That's very kind of ya! She's a beauty all right! She's a
cracker!

DAUGHTER. I believe there's problems with the Moore Street
shop, Maxie! People are saying ya won't make your
deadline of eleven o'clock! Do you want to comment on
that?

DAD. 'Sure that's a nonsense! That's just people talk! Are
people talking about that? Ya know the way that people love
the talk? Well that's all that is! That's people talking!
Talking their mouths off! That's all it is! She'll be open at
eleven all right boys! As sure as Sophia Loren has legs and
Marcus Enright's a prick that shop will be open!' They
laugh their journalistic laughs and lap me all down on their
tiny little pads. I make them me friends, in one smile taking
them all in. 'Now ya can follow me if ya like, lads, but I'm

off to Marlbora Street to see the next shop swing open its
doors on the delights of bedding, the practicalities of
Formica, the elegance of brushed draylon and the honesty
of pine! Onward!' I march away! Their rain-macks rustling
as they try to keep up with my pace!

DAD *and* DAUGHTER. Tickatocktickatocktickatocktickatock!
Eleven o'clock eleven o'clock eleven o'clock eleven o'clock
eleven o'clock eleven o'clock . . .

DAD. . . . spins about me brainbox! Spins around like a
bad friend, a scary ghost, a fucking devil of a time that is
eleven o'clock! Another corner rounded and there she is!
'Gentlemen, Maxie's Furniture Super Shop Number Three'.

Cameras flashing.

DAD. 'Jesus, but what a beautiful sight she is, lads, there with
her Pearly Gates open! (*Getting emotional.*) And when I
think of the little boy who used wash his one suit . . . one
fucking suit, mind you, each night to be clean in the
morning . . . ready for the work in the storeroom! Jesus lads
when I think of the thousands of cabinets and wardrobes
and three-piece suites at reasonable prices that have passed
through my life! When I think of the friends I have made . . .
the van men who've become family to me . . . D'you know
lads, but I have a charmed life! Like . . . like a fairyfuckingtale, lads. A fairyfuckingtale. 'Now onwards to Moore
Street and eleven o'clock!' By fuck that was a performance
worthy of honour! I didn't know I had it in me to be
emotional! Isn't life a box of surprises all the same?! The
walk feeling less powerful all of a sudden though, as I belt
up Henry Street with the Paparazzi on tow! I feel the nerves
twitching behind my eyes sending lumps into my throat like
shite blocking drains! Good fuck! I turn onto Moore Street
with all the grace of a milk cart with eleven o'clock ticking
into time and . . . ! (*He pauses and stares ahead his face
collapsing into failure, he whispers.*) Oh fuck. Oh Jesus.
(*He suddenly screams.*) 'BRIAN!! BRIAN YA LITTLE
FUCKER!! Is it not eleven o'clock and the doors still shut?!'

DAUGHTER. We're all over the place, boss!

DAD. 'Shut it! SHUT IT!! Shut your hole!!' I grabs hold of his hair and run! What's got into me?! I run through the shop smashing his head from wardrobe to table from cabinet to wall unit! I feel hair coming off in my fingers so I grab tighter! SCHLAPP!!! I take him to the office and open the door with his fucking head! SCHMAAAK! 'Ya little fucker! Make a fool a me will ya! We'll all have a laugh at Maxie, is that it!! Shmack! Schmack schmack! SCHMACK! SCHMACK! YA FAT BOLLIX!! YA FUCK! YA FUCK!' (*He stops. Cameras start to flash*) Flash flash flash flash FLASH!! I leave! I leave it all behind and leave! And leave Dublin! FLASH!! I see my newspaper picture bent over Brian and smashing his head ta mush! Fuck Dublin! Leave and drive! My last image a giant furniture shop with Marcus Enright and Sons gilded in gold! Fuck him! Fuck it! Fuck Dublin! FUCK!!

Last camera flashes loudly.

A pause. Can he continue?

DAUGHTER. And then what, Daddy?

DAD. And then I return to Cork and see the wife and see you . . . I see *you*. (*Hard.*) And I see yer fucked up body! I see how the polio has sent things wrong in *my* life! And I look at the wife who did this! What put it in my mind I can't say but I'm at the hardware shop and return to the house and I start building walls inside the house! Partition walls, ya know! And I make the space tight tight around you and yer Mam! WHAT SHAME YOU GAVE ME! And I spend the nights building the walls so it's tight tight tight and getting tighter! And during the day it's . . . Dan Dan!! *'Great to have ya back boss! Dublin was a bollix, I believe!'* Yerrah fuck, Dublin! *'Yer right boss!'* We'll get back to old times, Dan Dan! That will be great, hah? And we work our arses off! By fuck we're shifting stock around Cork like we were Santa Clauses! *'How's the daughter, Maxie!'* 'Sure my daughter's dead, Dan Dan! She died when I was up in Dublin! The Dublin cunts!' I get home in the evening with a car full of plasterboard and start at the walls! Thump pa thump pa thump pa thump pa thump pa

thump!! Your space getting tighter and tighter! I feed ya bits
of lunches I've robbed off Dan Dan! For a while I think of
killing ya straight off! But this seems the better option! Of
course it does!! Keep ya alive I can think of what to do
next! Nothing like a busy head! Nothing like options! Sure
that's business! Business is all about options! Keep your
options open and ya have choice! 'AND CHOICE IS LIFE!
Isn't that right Dan Dan?' *'Right as rain, boss!'* Thump pa
thump pa thump pa thump pa thump pa thump!! So I build
more and more and more walls! And one day a great big
wall I build right around this bed with you and yer Mam in!
Tight tight tight! Like a lunchbox with two humans at home
inside! It's perfect or something! 'A good year isn't it, Dan
Dan?!' 'A good year isn't it, Dan Dan?' 'Another good year
isn't it, Dan Dan!?' Ten years of good years, Dan Dan! Ten
years and the nightmare of Dublin has fucked off to
someone else entirely! Ten years of feeding wife and
daughter with Dan Dan's lunches! Ten years and the people
of Cork City FUCKING GENUFLECT in FRONT OF ME!
Now this! This is a life! Dan Dan! DAN DAN!! (*More
difficult now.*) You've got me on the van with ya today! I
read the pink docket and the name of Mrs. Dexter! A new
wall unit for the old bitch. 'No fucking mistakes now.' (*All
fearful.*) I grab holda my end of the wall unit and Dan Dan
has his, backing his way into Mrs. Dexters garden with her
lovely red roses. Look at the concentration swell Dan Dan's
brain. Little dribbles of sweat spit up on his fringe and edge
their way down his face. My head thumpathumpathumpa
thumpa thumpa! 'Easy Dan Dan! Watch it boy!' The strain
showing on Dan Dan's body the wall unit begins a nervous
shake. I look and stare into Dan Dan's eyes. And there . . .
there in Mrs. Dexter's garden . . . there with all my
customers peeping out through the curtains at the new wall
unit . . . there the nervous shake turns into a wobble and I
see the long fingers of Marcus Enright tipple . . . tipple . . .
tipple . . . tipple (*Long pause, then very controlled.*) Next
thing ya know my red face stands in the back of the van
with Dan Dan lifting bits of wall unit towards me. Him
crying like a baby. 'Step up here, Dan Dan.' And he does.
'I'm sorry, Maxie.' And I give him a smile as he turns away

and bends down to shift the broken wood. And my thumb
flicks the Stanley blade 'til all that's left is to slit Dan Dan's
throat! And I do. And I hold his head as my brainbox finally
explodes to the trickle of Dan Dan's blood doing their own
little funny race down his chest.

DAUGHTER. JESUS FUCK!! I get that tight tight tight in the
belly holding on to all the hate I have for you! I want to bite
and rip your fucking head off for that story you just blurted
out like a casual fart! Why? Jesus why the walls, you twisted
sad shit of a man! I remember only the house getting
smaller! I remember Mam whispering how we were in a
fairytale and how with a kiss one day the house would open
up! And open up back into space! And all the hammering
all through the night! Thump pa thump pa thump pa thump
pa thump pa thump!! Every night being pushed further and
further into the tight until both of us in the bed and the
hammering stops! AND THAT WAS YOU??! FUCKING
HELL!! Can shame sour so much? Was it shame that turned
to hate? It must have been hate! And we hold onto the
book! And she reads it and when she does she can find love
in her voice! And we stay awake . . . me and her. And I
can't sleep so she talks and talks! Sometimes not making
sense but sometimes making pictures with her words and
words become my life as I try to fill the space, for what
pictures do I really have but the four fucking walls that
you've given me, you fucker! And my head like a great big
lung at times so tight it could burst and other times let loose
on landscapes! Let free! And you hear me read and forget
the voice of my Mam and read fast . . . killing the romance
and making the landscapes so tight that they burst into
tears!! My life is a fucking rant and not the story I wish it to
be! I talk so fast so fast it's fucking killing the book and
killing me! And all from you from you from you from you!

He watches her for a bit and then calmly finishes his story.

DAD. I enter the house and into the maze of the partitions. I've
got the blood of Dan Dan on me hands. I make my way
through the maze of the plaster walls and see you crying on
the bed. I see Mam lying all hollow and dead like a doll.
When I lift her up you look at me. You don't know who

I am. And I take your Mam's body out. I walk through the maze with your crying fainter and fainter and the real world mixing up to louder and asking me out of the house. Your crying and the busy outside. And I stop. (*Pause.*) I stop and listen and what I hear is silence then. (*Long pause.*) And it's the first time in my life I've got room for silence. I stand with the tiny body of your Mam and let the silence clean me out for a bit. (*Pause.*) And then . . . and then it starts as a tiny thing in my mouth. I swallow it and it fills my stomach. And then my brain gets hold of it and it fills my everything. I have fear. It's fear. I'm afraid of my life outside. And I place your Mam on the ground and turn back until I arrive back at the bed. And I get into the bed and face you as I do now. And this is me talking. This is really me talking now. And I don't have words for you. I don't have the right words for you, love. I just want to sleep and get back to the silence but I can't.

He is overcome. The DAUGHTER *hands her* DAD *the book. He begins to read it. He reads slow. She calms and listens.*

DAD. A hush came over the vast ballroom as Katie stood at the top of the stairs. Her silken blond hair brushed gently off her bare shoulders as she made her descent. From the crowd, whispers passed from gentleman to lady. She was beautiful. Katie then walked through the crowd towards the man she had seen at church. Turning to her his heart began pounding. Could this be the same little girl who cycled so wildly around the village? She took his hand in hers. The man was shocked, and yet what could he do. Katie could feel the hard gaze of the audience watching her impertinence. She allowed it wash over her as she leaned towards him offering him her kiss. And when they kissed, everything that had gone before had been forgotten and everything in front of them was . . . was joy.

DAD *closes the book and looks at his* DAUGHTER.

Slowly the DAUGHTER *leans to her* DAD. *She kisses him softly on the forehead. He then kisses her . They sit back and look at each other. She listens to the silence for a bit.*

DAUGHTER. I'm in the bed. The panic is gone and all that's left is ta start over. I get that tiredness turn to calm . . . and I give in to sleep. I let go. Go.

The wall, which had crashed down, raises up and boxes them in once more as the lights fade off them.

Blackout.

The End.

misterman

Characters

MAMMY
THOMAS
EDEL

Lights on stage fade out. In the darkness we can hear someone walk onto the stage. They stop. There is silence for sometime. Sounds and noises of rumblings and explosions build to very loud. Suddenly a spotlight flicks on THOMAS, *a man in his mid-thirties.* THOMAS *replays the making and the beginning of the universe and mankind with much intensity.*

THOMAS. It all began from a Nothing. This loud crashing all began as a whisper but a whisper that was from God, from Him, from the Lord our Master . . . and that whisper grew and grew and became this growling and soon a thundering and a roaring that was never heard in the Nothing before. And out of the noise came a voice, the great voice of the Lord and he said 'Let there be light' . . . and on the Nothing a light shone. And what was the first light like? The light made the Nothing a Something which the Lord called Night and light was called Day. And He made the Earth and separated dry from wet to make the land and the sea, and He made vegetation and fruit and trees and covered the land in all colour and shone a bright yellow star to make the trees and plants grow and grow. And then a universe of smaller stars and other planets he set turning in the speckled light. And animals of all kinds and shapes they ran about the Earth and swam in the lovely blue seas that as a child I too would swim in. And God made us, Daddy told me. Man and Woman in his likeness to keep watch on what He had made. To be watching. To be watching. To be good. (*Pause.*) But Man and Woman's soul was not like God's soul because it was good and evil and evil it grew. It grew like that very first whisper but a whisper now of crying and suffering and it grew and is growing. And I'm watching because more and more people fill the Earth and little good and some little happiness is found. Because Man has forgotten God's words he gave us in Eden and His son we crucified him, we killed Him for offering us kind redemption and just carry on and on and on and sin has become our religion, greed our communion and now Evil . . . Evil is our God.

The sounds stop. A pause as THOMAS *watches the lights above him fade up.*

We can see that the sounds are coming from an old tape recorder slung over his shoulder. THOMAS *carries it and operates it throughout his story.*

THOMAS (*whispers up*). Everything is not good, Daddy. Daddy?

We hear his MAMMY*'s voice from the tape recorder.*

MAMMY. A scrambled egg is awful, Thomas? You used to take them boiled. What's the matter, my best boy in Ireland?

THOMAS (*all business*). Tomorrow they'll be boiled again. It's like eating yellow spit off a soggy bit of toast.

MAMMY. Stick with what ya know!

THOMAS. I thought I might visit Daddy at the cemetery. I got some blue lilacs and lined the rim. Got a new bit of that gravel green stuff as well. I made a map of Ireland in the centre with the gravel. It looks like Ireland on the grave with the sea surrounding it.

MAMMY. That's nice. I think it's great you like flowers, Thomas. It's a nice side to your character.

Finishing his eggs. Closes his eyes and says a short prayer.

THOMAS. Lord watch over your humble servant keeping his soul clean, his spirit strong, through Christ our Lord, Amen. Right . . . best make a start!!

MAMMY. You might give me a rub with the Vicks when you get back from your travels?

THOMAS. I heard you coughing all night, d'ya know. It's not too good, Mammy. Like an old engine. Chugging away there, good style! Like a steam train, Mammy! Like a little old choo choo!!

MAMMY (*laughing*). Oh a little old choo choo!

THOMAS. I'll look after you Mammy don't worry about that.

MAMMY. Off with you then, Mister Traveller. Get me a surprise from Centra, Thomas. A sugary surprise, Thomas. You know, what I'd like, love.

THOMAS. Bye Mammy.

Sound of the outside from the tape recorder. THOMAS *appearing tentative and nervous of the World.*

THOMAS. I feel the front door's gentle shove behind me as I step out into Inishfree. Thoughts of the Universe and the phlegmy basin that sits under Mammy's bed, belting about my head with a mad swishy swish. The Lord God at my side, the day open and big.

(*He adopts a suitable voice for Mrs. O' Leary.*) 'Oh the cold Thomas?'

Oh are ya full of it Mrs. O' Leary?

'Sure once I get it into my body it's very difficult to get the thing out, Thomas. Try as I might the cold just sits inside and won't budge an inch. And sure look at me with my old chalky bones like crack crackers. But I wrap them up, Thomas! And you love, going out for a walk are ya?'

I am! Off out for, Mammy! Got to keep her in the biscuits!

'Oh she loves her biscuits, doesn't she!? Mad about them biscuits!'

She loves her biscuits all right.

'You're a fine son to her, Thomas! Oh for God's sake when I think of my own son, Timmy!! When I think of, Thomas, with his disco nights and the way he'd bark at me like I was a black slave or something. I walked into his room the other evening and I'm not having ya on when I say a bomb had been let off . . . and then the smell, Thomas . . . well what with the bomb and then the stink . . .'

Was it terrible, tell me?

'Terrible isn't the word, Thomas! Sure I was scrubbing for days. Hands torn to shreds by the Harpic. Look at them. Pigeon's feet, Thomas.'

Well that's not on, Mrs. O' Leary. Sure who brought us into the world only our mothers . . . 'Children be obedient to your parents in the Lord' . . . that is what uprightness demands. The first Commandment that has a promise attached to it is 'Honour your father and mother' and the promise is; so that you may have a long life and prosper in the land'. If you can't wake on the Lord's day and tidy away the odd pair of underpants, if it is not in your spirit to say that the spuds were lovely and that the meat was tender . . . if your parents, Mrs. O' Leary are given the same respect as a mangey dog would be given . . . well in my book you're not even fit for pig fodder. Look you send Timmy around my way and I'll have a word in his ear! (*Pause.*)

'D'ya know what I'd do if I didn't have my senses? I'd kidnap ya, ya little treasure!!'

Ahhh now, Mrs. O' Leary, stop it!!!!

'No I would!! I would kidnap ya, Thomas!! That's what I'd do. Yer a little dotey!'

Bye now Mrs. O' Leary. Take care of yourself! (*Takes out a small notebook and writes.*) Timmy O' Leary. Cleanliness.

(*Adopts the voice of the formidable Charlie.*) 'Thomas!'

Mr. Mc Anerny.

'Dull ol' day, isn't it?'

Well it will brighten up hopefully!

'D'you think it will brighten up, Mister Weather-man?'

Well it might.

'I don't think it will, ya know!!'

Well it might or it mightened who's to say.

'I'd say you'd be better putting your money on the 'mightened'. I'd say that's where the wise money's going, Thomas!'

Well I suppose we'll see the outcome soon enough, Charlie.

'We will see soon. Of course we'll see the outcome soon enough ya can always count on that one, God willing. Off on your little walk then?'

Off to visit the cemetery, actually.

'Your poor dad. Now he was great man. Great man. Best shop in town, wasn't it Thomas? What a variety! A selection! And for those days. I mean bananas are two a penny now, of course! But back then when your Dad was your age sure people would travel to see the variety. Imagine saying that people would travel to see a banana. Sounds bonkers but that's the truth. That's the world's truth!! Travelling to see a banana. That's where we're off to! We're off to see a banana from the jungles!! Word will get around of the soft yellow fruit that was selling in Magill's Grocery and lines . . . I mean lines of people talking and laughing over this funny old bendy banana thing and all the people with the bendy banana grin on their old pusses, laughing and giggling away like happy monkeys . . .'

I stop listening to old chatterbox Charlie Mc Anerny and look up. I look up to where I want to be, ta tell yas the truth. Up there safe in the clouds and far away from Inishfree.

Heavenly music. THOMAS *goes up to Heaven.*

THOMAS. I sit like an angel of goodness up here! Sit in the bluey white making me invisible. I listen to God's music soothing and piercing me with His goodness. No more the smart words of Charlie Mc Anerny digging into me. My head now free and without pain. I'm in a place where other's speak is like poetry too. A place where I belong. I see other faces surrounding me. Beautiful and kind they welcome Thomas. Angels all of us as we sit amongst the clouds. I have a look down on Inishfree. My town. (*Pause.*) And I see its pure white soul being stained by the bad. I see the goodness being chased out of people's faces. I look how temptation has twisted its ugly way into my neighbours . . . like they were blind and playing at the gates of Hell they look. I get a tightness all of a sudden like some sort of sadness making me want to puke. But I watch it change. The good angel makes it change. A bright light of goodness making the pure grow again. Like that first Eden, Thomas. And God places his hand around my shoulder. Inishfree saved from the terrible wrath of fire and brimstone. Saved by compassion and a real love. And me and God smile and look down on all my good work. It's going to be such a beautiful place, Lord.

THOMAS *comes down from Heaven.*

THOMAS. Such a beautiful place. (*Slight pause.*) Bye now Mr. Mc Anerny! God bless!

THOMAS *kneels down. He is at his Daddy's grave.*

THOMAS. Hello Daddy, it's only me, Thomas! Just popped by to check in. I brought ya these flowers. The graves looking smashing by the way! It's the best of the lot, I'd say! What do you make of the gravel map of Ireland? Dynamite, isn't it?! A good joke. A-one! Billy Traynor got himself a new car, Daddy! Who's to say there's no money in shovelling! He's proud as punch just like the fella on the Lotto ad! Will ya ever forget the day ya caught him pinching the news-paper in the shop, Daddy? Ya gave him an awful hiding that day! He was in bits that night in Boyle's! Pouring the pints inta him to ease the pain! Billy's only an old fecker anyway! Everyone knows that. I really miss ya, Daddy. But I'm doing my best with it and I bet you'd be proud of the work I'm doing about town. It's just funny not having the shop and it being so quiet about the house with Mammy and me and Trixie. The swelling's gone down after the kittens, by the way. Mammy asked me to drown three of them and keep the best one. Best to drown the lot, I said. Being an only child is tough . . . being an only kitten must be a terrible curse though. It really must.

A pause.

THOMAS (*he adopts a man's voice*). 'But they're creepy old places aren't they, Tommy? Gives me the creeps just work-ing beside the thing. God he was a great man, wasn't he?'

You wouldn't be able to call many people great but my Daddy was great, all right.

'Will ya have a cuppa with me? I've got the kettle on in the garage.'

Well that's awfully Christian of you, Eamon!

'Now watch your good clothes on that old banger there, Tommy! Grab a seat where ya can right. Hope ya like it strong. Me I like my tea like tar. Unless ya can trod on the stuff it's useless, boy!' (*Laughs.*)

Sure once it's wet and warmish it's no bother to me. (*Pause.*) My God, what a collection of cars! (*Tentative.*) But ya know Eamon . . . I can't see the attraction in travelling at all! People whizzing from A to B and not spending enough time having a good look around, do you know what I mean?

'I don't Tommy, but ya plan ta tell me all the same no doubt!'

Ah I won't go boring ya now, Eamon. It's just it seems to me that people are filling their lives with unnecessary entertainment when the Lord has provided everything that is needed already. If time wasn't always spent in life's fast lane people would see the simple beauty of the Lord. Do you know what I mean by that?

'I don't Tommy, sorry!'

Well . . . well have you ever worried that one day you'll wake up and forget about all what the Lord has done for us? That the sunrise and the changing seasons won't surprise you anymore. That people, Eamon . . . man and woman would be something to be just used and not seen as a creation of the Lord God which deserve kindness and respect. We were given such a great gift, Eamon. It's this arrogance that some people have. All the Lord wants is us to love Him as He loves us. To return His love and to love each other. Why is that so difficult, Eamon? When the Lord is not the first thing in your life it is not a life. Love and respect the Lord God and Heaven will be your eternal home. It's that simple.

'You're a walking saint, Tommy! The whole town's saying it, son!! No doubt about it but you're well touched?'

Touched?

'By the man Himself is what I mean?'

Well a prophet of God needs a following, Eamon. I understand that you have your hands full in the garage and with the hurling team but but I've always felt that you've understood . . . that you understand my work . . . that there's a bond, maybe, between us. If you were to work alongside me. Now I would work you hard but fair. We would call on people together. Put right where there is wrong. Comfort where there is loneliness or sadness. God's work is hard but the rewards, Eamon, are so great, ya know!

'That's kind of you to ask me, Tommy! I'd have to talk it over with Mary though. I wouldn't want to take it lightly. I'd put in one hundred per cent for the man upstairs you know that. Y'all have a hot sup?!'

I will thanks! Lash it in there, Eamon!! Thank you. God bless. (*Pause. Thomas then sees something on the wall.*) Is that what I think it is?

'Ah don't be looking at that Tommy! Sure tell me more.'

But that Eamon . . . that is filth! How any woman can strip off and allow that sort of thing. And you? Oh good God but you get satisfaction from some dirty prostitute stuck there for your sad relief! Well this is not good, Eamon! I took you as my ally and not some sick pervert man! But guess who's been led on the big merry-go-round!! Who's the big eegit only Thomas Magill!!

'Ah now take it easy, Tommy! Look there's no harm being done!'

(*Losing it.*) No harm!? No harm?! Is it not Satan's Black Angel right in front of me then! Well stop the rot stop the rot!! Before I know it, you'll all be at it! Let me out of here!?

'Ah Tommy, for crying out loud!'

My name is Thomas!! My name is Thomas! My name is
Thomas! My name is Thomas! And I run and run fast up
over the hill! My good words sent burning about me.
Inishfree once more all bad and diseased. My legs unable
to climb to Heaven are stuck still in the Devil's land. In
Sodom, good Christ!! In Sodom!! And run Thomas run!
Turn back and see Eamon Moran standing at his garage
door . . . his eyes a piercing red, his ragged wings lit by
fire! (*Screams out.*) Lord God take by my hand and lead
me out of this festering pit! This Hell!! Save me Lord and
place me sitting by your side! Save me Lord Almighty!!
Save me!!

A dog starts barking. THOMAS *stops. The dog seems to be
approaching him.* THOMAS *is terrified and slowly backs
away.*

Dog is faded up to very loud. THOMAS *freaks out with
punches and kicking.* THOMAS *turns off the tape recorder.
The dog stops.*

New state. Sounds of quiet café from the tape recorder.

THOMAS. It wouldn't be everyday that I'd give myself a treat
like this one but today I'm having a cheesecake, definitely!
Mrs. Cleary's Café . . . the red chequered tablecloths all
bright and breezy. Cheese? Cake? How anyone could think
that a whisked bit of cheese with a broken biscuit base
could set the baking world on fire . . . they must have been
(*Introducing.*) And here she is!! The Ban an Ti (*Puts on the
voice of Mrs. Cleary.*)

'Ahh Thomas but you're looking fabulous! What a rig-out!
It's top, it really is!! Oh look at ya, ya've grown up to be a
fine looking fella! Best catch in Inishfree, they say! Ladies
are ya all right for the tea? Yee are!! That's fabulous that is
and isn't Mrs. Heffernan looking like a new model with her
hair-do done up on her head like a hairy fairy cake, if there
is such a thing!! A hairy fairy cake? Not in my little café!
Not on your Nellie oh no!! Wooooooo would ya look at his

lovely neat feet! Stuck there in those little shoes! I bet
you're a dancer, hey Thomas! I bet you're a dancer? Fred
Astaire had feet the picture of those fellas! Grab a hold of
Mrs. Cleary and we'll have an old waltz for ourselves!'

I've just come in for a cheesecake, Mrs Cleary!

'What?! And you've no time for a dance!? Are ya shy?
You're not shy are ya!? Sure that's a nonsense! Up and
we'll have a turn around the floor! Tonight's the community
dance, Thomas, have ya forgotten love?! We'll get in some
practice and show the whole town, won't we?! We'll show
those old codgers a little bit of Fred and Ginger's still going
strong as ya like in sad old Inishfree. Of course it is ya little
dancer!! Dancing dancing ohhh the little dancer dancing
there in his dancing leprechaun dancing shoes!!'

Look if you don't mind!! (*Quite terrified.*) I mean, if it's
all right with you, I'd rather not dance, you know! All I
want is some cheesecake. I mean, if it's all right with you
Mrs. Cleary I'd like a bit of your fabulous cheesecake .
If that's all right now, Mrs. Cleary! (*Pause.*) Ya can't be
allowed to be seen dancing in the Café least of all with
Mrs. Cleary. Ya can never tell if the rumours are true but if
they are there's quite a few farmers around Inishfree who've
taken to the old whisked cheese and broken biscuit base,
if ya get me meaning! Thanks very much, Mrs. Cleary.
Magnificent . . . magnificence!

THOMAS *eats his cheesecake. Sound of the door being
opened and a bell sound.* THOMAS *turns towards it.
Immediately he is mesmerised at what he sees.*

THOMAS. And then something walks into my life. A vision
with pale skin and her eyes green. She smiles at me as her
dress blue brushes by my hand. By the back of my hand.
I feel the tiny hairs on my fist tickle and stretch out, ya
know the way they do. She catches my look sending me
blushing and turning away. An angel, Thomas! An angel.
Jaynee I feel weak all of a sudden. My back to her. Almost
resting to her. I feel ashamed then. Can't figure out why.
Her grace and beauty, I suppose. So beautiful and pure.
I listen to her at the counter. The life in her voice. The ease

and humour of her words. Only her words, sounding of
Summer sunshine. (*Pause.*) And then I see Eamon Moran's
grabbing hands as my hands . . . as large and gluttonous as
that whore Mrs. Cleary. In front of this goodness everything
is filth. Everything, Thomas.

The bell sounds again. THOMAS *gets up and scrubs his
hands with a paper napkin. He leaves after her.*

THOMAS. And there she is! She stands outside Centra
watching me. She stands amongst little girls who poke her
sides and make her giggle. She looks at me, her mouth
curving, her eyes all a sparkle, her body caught in shyness
twitching ta turn around. She looks at me and turns and her
blond ringlets spring and bounce to her shoulder. (*Pause.*)
And I'm back in the bluey white of the clouds and Heaven
filled with angels with bow an' arrows and cheeky faces.
And she looks at me and asks, 'What's happened to
'respect', Thomas?' And I say, 'Respect's now just a word,
angel!' 'What's happened to love?' I ask her. And she
whispers, 'Teach me'.

New state.

THOMAS. I'll take these Jammy Dodgers off ya, Mrs.
Pearson! (*He turns to someone who says hello to him.*)
Ohh hello! (*Slight pause.*) No these are for my, Mammy,
actually! (*Slight pause.*) No I wasn't looking at you,
honestly! Well maybe I was? Did you mind that I was it's
just . . . well to see somebody like you down here . . . I'm
sorry for staring at you? (*Pause.*) Thomas, that's right!
(*Slight pause.*) And you are . . . ? Edel. (*Pause.*) Well I do
the Lord's work as you know . . . but . . . Well I walk . . . as
exercise for body and soul, you know . . . it's . . . (*Pause.*)
I don't suppose you'd like to join me on one of me walks,
Edel? (*Pause.*) Outside Boyles? Here! Great!! At two?! So
I'll see you here at four then!! See you then!! (*Pause. He
'leaves the shop'.*)

(*The nasty voice of Mrs. O' Donnell.*) 'And what has you all
pleased with yourself? You should be ashamed. I knew
when I heard it. Mrs. Cleary said it wasn't possible but
when Eamon Moran told me what you did. Christ it's the

sort of thing you expect from a teenager. You punched him
to bits. He's fucking dead, Thomas! To see little Roger's
body tipped on the side of the road like old rubbish. When
my Marty hears what you've done he'll knock twelve
shades of shit right out of you, believe me boy! What would
your mother think of that sort of carry on. Are you listening
to what I'm saying you mad fucking eegit!?'

(*Struggling.*) I am listening Mrs. O' Donnell but to be
honest yer making very little sense! Sure wasn't it yer dog
who took the first bite?

'But to kick the poor creature to death! Good Christ, man!'

Nobody is as sorry as me, Mrs. O' Donnell! But in fairness
it was either my boots or the vet's gun! It made little
difference! The poor doggy didn't have a bright future once
he bit me, now be honest, did he? (*Slight pause.*)

'Jesus Christ, Thomas Magill! What are we going to do
with you?' (*She cries.*)

I watch Mrs. O' Donnell carry her tears down the road and
disappear into the grey. Take a deep breath feeling my soul
lighten and try to ease. And that's when it starts, ya know!
The grey clouds gather above and start to spin . . . and God
spins them for my entertainment! And they spin so fast I
feel almost sucked up by them! Like I'm being sucked up
by a giant hoover and sent to somewhere beautiful!
Somewhere where the angels walk hand in hand.
Somewhere good, Thomas!

Enormous sounds as THOMAS *thrusts the Jammy Dodgers
into the air in triumph.*

New state.

THOMAS. Time to take your top off, Mammy. (*To audience.*)
The Vick begins to lift little clouds of doubt that often
wander into my head. And I can really see the happy destiny
of Inishfree being painted by me and her, the Angel Edel.
It's all beginning to turn, you see . . . goodness has found a
new strength it seems. I can feel it.

MAMMY. Thanks Thomas! You're a great little healer. Great healing hands, God bless them.

THOMAS. Sitting over a gas heater doesn't help your breathing, Mammy, I've said it once and I'll say it again.

MAMMY. Oh but it gets awfully cold, Thomas.

THOMAS. I think you'll find that putting on some extra clothes will sort you out there. It doesn't take a brainbox to figure that one out, Mammy.

MAMMY. I'm sorry, Thomas.

THOMAS. All I'm doing is asking you to throw an extra jumper on. It's not like I'm asking you to fetch me a packet of biscuits from the shop.

MAMMY. All right, Thomas.

THOMAS. Look Mammy, I think a little more understanding is needed here. I'm looking after both our interests. Your sore cough and me wasting God's good time spreading the Vick on. I'm asking you to do something that even you could manage, Mammy! A jumper, that's all! An extra jumper! Give me one less thing to be worried about. I mean, do you have any idea of the day I've put down? Now a little bit more co-operation would be appreciated. It would make my work a lot easier to come home to a happy home, Mammy. I'm not asking for much but when I come through that door well what I expect . . . what I am looking for is respect. The same respect that you showed Daddy.

MAMMY. Why Thomas?

THOMAS. Ahhh Mammy! You're not being very bright today, are ya? Do I have to spell it out to you?

MAMMY. Stop, Thomas!

THOMAS (*screams*). What? You stupid woman. Have you understood anything I have said?! Just put on a jumper! Have you any idea of the cost!? The gas bill, Mammy!! You will not ruin my work woman!! Are you listening to me?! Look just do it!!

THOMAS *grooms himself for going out. New state.*

THOMAS. Hello Edel!! Right on time! It's a beautiful day, all
right. (*Slight pause.*) So ahh . . . shall we? (*To audience.*)
We walk. Her all lively and laughing. We cut a glowing line
through the grey road of Inishfree, her almost skipping a
dance so full of the happy she is. We see some teenage girls
who point and laugh at us making her giggle even more.
I listen to her big laugh. Fills me with God's light it does.
I'm almost trotting behind . . . so fast and speedy she walks.
That glow about her . . . a halo . . . the Holy Spirit shining
from her making her almost invisible to me in the sunshine.
Oh thank you Lord. She hops over a gate and off through
Friel's field tiptoeing through the lazy cattle and poo poo.
I do the same. I catch up with her by the river.

River sounds from the tape recorder.

THOMAS. You know when I was a boy I used to come here,
Edel and fish for brown trout with my Daddy on Sundays.
On Saturdays I'd build dams in the shallow parts of the river
so that on the Sundays we'd nearly always find a fat trout
stuck in one of the dams. On one Sunday we came back to
Mammy as proud as punch. in the brown paper bag was a
big salmon, a huge fella. He was well stuck in the walls of
one of the dams, ya see. Daddy hushed him out and
whacked him against the trunk of that tree there, splaying
his innards everywhere. Anyway, Mammy gutted and
cleaned him out and we must have had three cutlets each.
Like royalty Daddy said. But then the next Sunday we went
fishing we came back with a brown trout like we did
usually. The trouble was we couldn't eat that trout. A taste
of the salmon had put us off the poor brown trout
completely. (*Pause.*) You understand what I mean by that
story don't you Edel? You can understand the good word
like I do. Isn't that right angel? (*Slight pause.*) She stays
quiet. Time to stop yabbering on I stay quiet for a bit
myself. (*Long pause.*) I want to reach out and hold her
hand. I want her to love me. Her hair smells of coconuts or
something. Her fingers tearing fat grass to thin. I want to
hold my Angel Edel's hand and touch Heaven. (*Slight
pause.*) Edel, do you mind if I hold your hand?

*Thunder and sound of torrential rain. The stage is drenched
in rain as is* THOMAS. THOMAS *walks through the town.
He is furious and very hurt.*

THOMAS. Not for the first time God roars down on Inishfree!
I walk in the rain with its tracks pouring down my face and
drenching my heavy soul. I hear someone bark and then
laugh! Laughing at me!! Will I ever be free from those
laughs?! Walk on Thomas! I'm feeling the whole town sit
hard on my back and wanting to drag me down to their level.
'God saw that human wickedness was great on Earth and
that human hearts contrived nothing but wicked schemes all
day long. God regretted having made human beings on
Earth and was grieved at heart. And God said, "I shall rid
the surface of the Earth of the human beings whom I
created – human and animal, the creeping things and the
birds of Heaven – for I regret having made them." But Noah
won God's favour. Noah was a good man, an upright man
among his contemporaries, and Noah walked with God.'
I'll take these Jammy Dodgers off you, Mrs Pearson.

Back in the rain. THOMAS *starts barking wildly. He laughs
as he sees something.*

THOMAS. I see some man outside my house with his thumb
stuck to the doorbell, his face furious from the long wait.
Mammy sat inside like the Queen Mother herself! (*Laughs.
Stops.*) What did I do? What did I do? He turns and walks
fast towards me, yelling about his dead dog Roger! It's me
he wants, it's me he wants!! Oh Christ, please, no!! No No
NO!! DON'T DON'T!!

THOMAS *is struck on the face and falls to the ground. He
splashes violently on the soaked ground screaming like a
child. Sounds stop and* THOMAS *lies crying loudly. He
stands and roars at the town.*

*We hear Doris Day singing 'It's time to say Goodnight.'
During it* THOMAS *undresses out of his wet clothes to his
underpants. His body is heavily bruised. The song comes to
an end.* THOMAS *looks up to a suit which is hanging in the
house. He calls to it, 'Daddy'. He takes it down gently and
begins to dress in this new suit. As he does it is clear that he*

*is being filled by a new confidence. And yet during the
dialogue below* THOMAS *is appearing to crack. We hear
his* MAMMY.

MAMMY. Doris Day did for baby pink what De Valera did for
black, Thomas. She's a beauty, isn't she! I'd love to have a
cup of tea and a biscuit with Doris. She doesn't look like a
Jammy Dodger sort of woman. Of course that's no reason
not to like her. More of a Lemon Puff lady really. How's the
river looking, Thomas?

THOMAS. Great. It's still nice. Much the same as it always
has been, Mammy.

MAMMY. Ahh good, sure no news is good news. You're off
out, I suppose?

THOMAS. The community dance is on in the hall. I thought
I'd show my face to them, ya know!

MAMMY. Good boy! Sure there's no point being locked up in
here with your Mammy all this time.

THOMAS. Sure I don't mind that! I got ya another packet of
Jammy Dodgers. I left them on the press in the kitchen. Just
in case you run out, ya know.

MAMMY. You're so good to me son. I love ya, son, I really do.

THOMAS. I don't know what sort of creature I'd be without
ya, Mammy. It seems like we've nearly got it all sewn up in
here. Almost. If I wish it strong enough I can sort of see my
Daddy next to you on the couch watching the quiz shows on
the telly and I'd be sitting by his feet. Sometimes I feel that
love's gone on holidays, that somehow it slipped out the
front door to another place entirely, Mammy. (*Pause.*) I'll be
home late I'd say. I'll be dead quiet though.

MAMMY. You've something on yer mind, Thomas?

THOMAS. No no. (*Pause.*) Sweet dreams, Mammy.

THOMAS *leaves. We hear the distorted sounds of rain,
traffic and a crowd from his tape recorder.*

THOMAS. I feel the front door's gentle shove as I step out
into Inishfree. My town. I look across the road as they

queue to get inside the school hall. I see Mick Barry relieve
himself against our house and I think of what would have
been me tomorrow on the cold hard ground scrubbing his
memory from our home. (*Pause.*) I see Eamon Moran and
his tiny wife ahead of me in the queue. He looks at me.
I watch them laugh as he pulls funny faces. Then Mrs
O'Donnell and her husband come over to join in. I watch
as he replays my beating, doing the face of a crying baba.
The face of Thomas. All I can see is the emptiness inside
them. Their life scooped out from them. Now I feel nothing
for them. (*Pause.*) There is a town where angels from
Heaven come to stay on Earth. There is a great love
between all men and women there. A respect, a kindness.
Just a light warm wind is felt through the town as the river
pops and gurgles with ease and playfulness. There are no
wicked tricks. Words are pure. There is only goodness.
(*Pause.*) The queue begins its shuffle into the inside. There's
so much that has to be said to these people. And I feel
God's strength building me up and holding my hand as
I walk down . . . down into Hell.

THOMAS *enters into the sound of a packed hall, people
dancing, singing, chatting. He stands on a chair and faces
the community and gathers all his confidence.*

THOMAS (*he announces*). Is it me or is everything cracked?!
I've tried my best for every one of you. I've done my very
best. I know that and so does God! I've even taken on your
laughs because I once believed that you had some goodness
inside. I wanted to believe it so much. Do you know we
could have made God so proud of Inishfree if only you had
listened . . . but like me God's heart is torn apart with the
disappointment of what's happened down here. Those who
I watched sin I was still willing to offer some guidance.
Some direction to God, wasn't I?! But today you tricked
me. Taking advantage of my search for love and goodness,
isn't that right?! You had me believing that the Lord had
sent me a companion . . . an Angel. I'd say you all had a
good laugh tonight in Boyle's, did you?! All over Thomas
Magill and his mockyah Angel! Well the Devil has had his
last day in Inishfree, make no mistake! (*Long pause.*) When

my Daddy died and we lost the shop, what were me and
Mammy to you? We were nothing. You gave us no respect.
Well listen to this now! We are the ones who are going to be
saved! Do you hear that?! God said to me, 'Come back up
to Heaven, Thomas! Your good work has been ignored as
was my son's work! Join your Daddy! Your Mammy will be
saved for she was the Mother of Righteousness! Leave
Inishfree, Thomas! Leave them to die!' And I will go up to
Heaven and sit beside the Lord and Daddy . . . and we will
wait for Mammy's good soul to rise above the clouds . . .
and we will make a new world . . . and I will forget you.
It's too late to repent by the way. How many times have
I listened to you when you had no one to talk to? When
I offered you the chance of redemption it was you who
tricked and tempted me with that false love. It is far too
late!! 'For he who sows to his own flesh will from the flesh
reap corruption?' My heart still holds some regret for what
we might have made together . . . but I am stronger and
I will watch you die . . . because you are not God's friends.
You are the Devil's friends.

*The sounds of the hall continue. Perhaps they didn't even
hear him.*

Long pause. Silence. Heaven.

THOMAS. And words make way for silence and space in my
head. And angels come down, and bring a cloud and I step
onto the cloud. And I watch the school hall ceiling open . . .
as I'm raised higher and higher, the clouds spinning,
Heaven sucking me up like a great big hoover. And I feel an
Angel at my shoulder. She hands me a burning torch. And I
have a look down on Inishfree and I can see the goodness of
what I'm doing. I let go of the torch and I listen as the lost
souls of Inishfree, burn in Hell beneath us.

The stage goes up in flames around.

THOMAS. And we're alone in the fluffy blue white of the
clouds, me and you. 'Do you mind if I hold your hand?'

THOMAS *operates the tape recorder and we hear the
sounds of* EDEL *and* THOMAS *down by the river.*

THOMAS. Do you mind if I hold your hand, Edel.

EDEL. Fuck off, Thomas!

THOMAS. I just want ta hold yer hand, that's all!

EDEL. What the fuck are you doing!?

THOMAS. Please, Edel!

EDEL. Let go, ya fucking moran!

EDEL is heard struggling with THOMAS. *She screams.*
THOMAS *is in Heaven listening to it.*

THOMAS *is heard hitting her. She screams again. We hear*
THOMAS *smashing her head with a rock over and over. He*
listens to it for some time.

Content that he has done the right thing THOMAS *turns*
EDEL'*s screaming off.*

He faces his 'imaginary angel', losing himself back in the
pretend.

THOMAS. Can I kiss your hand now? Everything is so right.
Such goodness. Like a great big happy book. Because
nobody's listening. Nobody's listening. Nobody's listening
to us.

THOMAS *kissses 'her hand'.*

Lights remain on THOMAS *as he sits happily in Heaven.*

The lights fade out to black as the stage continues to burn
around THOMAS.

The End.